"If your actions inspire others to dream more, learn more, do more and become more, you are a leader."

John Quincy Adams

Dedicated to Charissa, Saatchi and Keaton.

CONTENTS

Dedication   1

Introduction   5

Chapter 1. Get personal with your team   9

Chapter 2. Trust and be trustworthy   16

Chapter 3. Ensure everyone on the team has a   25
voice at the table

Chapter 4. Leave titles and egos at the door   31

Chapter 5. Level the playing field   38

Chapter 6. Understand what motivates your   42
team

Chapter 7. How you communicate matters   52
more than ever

Chapter 8. Go the extra mile to hire the best   55
talent

Chapter 9. Final Advice. Look after people on   60
the way up

References   64

About The Author   67

INTRODUCTION

As a rising star in the organisation, the decision to promote you will have come as little surprise to your teammates and colleagues.

Time and time again you've demonstrated the ability to deliver high-quality work, consistently delivering value for your team and the company. You're the person everyone turns to when the team is confronted with difficult issues and the one they trust to lead the most complex projects.

Your reputation for professionalism and resilience under pressure precedes you, not to mention your unwavering dedication and commitment to the success of the team. You have become a role model for others in the team, who regularly seek out your counsel and guidance.

The celebrations, however, are soon short-lived, and after a brief honeymoon period, the reality of your new responsibilities starts to sink in. It's as if, almost overnight, expectations of you have completely changed, and the spotlight that has been shining on you just got much brighter.

There is a whole new set of dynamics and unwritten rules between you and your team. Your once teammates and peers now report in to you and see you through a different lens. Your influence on their career ambitions and goals just got significantly more pronounced.

You now set the tone for the kind of culture the team will experience, which will either be one of trust, collaboration, motivation and belonging or one filled with mistrust, dysfunction, and individualism.

As a leader in 2020, how you show up every day. The choices you make. What you say. How you respond in the good times and during those challenging periods. All these things will determine your impact as a leader, and the performance and fulfillment of your team.

Equally as important, these things will influence the kind of leader that your team will either one day aspire to be, or one that they will avoid becoming at all costs.

What value will this book bring you?

Inspired by some of the world's leading thinkers from the fields of psychology, neuroscience, leadership development and team performance, the purpose of this book is to serve as a guide for individuals that have taken on new or growing leadership responsibilities.

Told through a collection of short stories and anecdotes, readers will be equipped with a more informed understanding of what drives individual and team behaviour, supported by practical advice on how to cultivate a team culture of trust, belonging and performance.

Personally, as a fan of the coffee break read, this book has been written to cater for those looking for a quick but value packed read.

It is intended to serve as your leadership reference guide. As new challenges and situations arise, the principles and practical interventions shared in the book are to be revisited throughout your progression as a new and developing leader.

The book also includes references to a number of additional resources that inspired this book and will enable readers to continue on their knowledge and development journeys. Examples include book recommendations from bestselling authors on the topic of leadership development, high-performing teams and cultures; inspiring TED talks that have been viewed by millions the world over; as well as thought leadership papers and articles written by leading behavioural and neuroscience academics.

CHAPTER 1. GET PERSONAL WITH YOUR TEAM

U nless you'd worked in Silicon Valley, few people would have recognised the name Bill Campbell. At least not until the book Trillion Dollar Coach was published in 2019, which tells the story of his life from the vantage points of the three authors Eric Schmidt, Jonathan Rosenberg, and Alan Eagle who were all coached by Bill whilst senior executives at Google.

A former American college football player and coach, Campbell went on to coach and mentor many of Silicon Valley's tech visionaries including Steve Jobs (Apple co-founder), Larry Page (co-founder of Google) and Eric Smidt (former Google CEO), as well as other executives from other tech powerhouses such as Twitter and eBay.

Trillion Dollar Coach is a book based on interviews with over 80 people who knew Bill and details many of his coaching principles that have been applied successfully to help business leaders and managers create high-performing teams and organisations. Since his death in 2016, many of Bill's leadership principles and interventions have been adopted by Google to help new and seasoned leaders within the company.

One of these interventions is described as the "Trip Report". It was a ritual where leaders would spend a few minutes at the start of their team meetings discussing what everyone got up to during the weekend. Everyone would reveal to their colleagues a glimpse of their lives outside of the workplace.

Not only did this ritual allow team members to learn a little more about each other on a more personal level, it served the purpose of everyone being engaged in the discussion right from the very start, laying the foundations for strengthened working relationships.

Behavioural science explains this through the *neutral coupling effect*, where sharing personal stories strengthens the cognitive connections between two people, in turn increasing the probability that they will work well together.

Advice. Create your own team version of the Trip Report

From time to time, taking the opportunity to spend a few minutes at the beginning of a meeting to invite your team members to speak about a topic outside of work is a powerful way of building empathy, rapport and trust within the team.

It also serves as a nice reminder for everyone on the team that their teammates have a life outside of the workplace. It brings a *just like me* perspective where they are reminded that others have hobbies, family and friends *just like me*, as well as hopes, anxieties and vulnerabilities *just like me*.

Encouraging regular disclosure of non-intrusive personal details creates stronger empathy and in turn trust between a leader and her team. It allows the team to see each other through a more human lens and build a stronger connection.

In Patrick Lencioni's New York bestselling 2002 book (*The Five Dysfunctions of a Team*) he highlights six non-intrusive questions that leaders can use to start to build rapport and empathy with their teams.

1. Your hometown
2. Number of kids in the family
3. Interesting childhood hobbies
4. Biggest challenge growing up
5. First job
6. Worst Job

Advice. Build "social sensitivity" in the team

The direct correlation between levels of empathy and team performance was on show in one of the largest studies of team performance ever done.

In 2016, the *New York Times Magazine* covered an in-depth look into the significant undertaking that Google went through to try to figure out why some teams excelled whilst others struggled to perform. Code named *Project Aristotle*, Google's leading experts from the fields of organisational psychology, sociology and statistics analysed the structures, dynamics and behaviours of over 180 teams in the company.

Article: "What Google Learned from Its Quest to Build the Perfect Team"

As covered in the article, one of the key observations from the study was that members of high-performing Google teams consistently showed higher levels of average social sensitivity. This was the ability to interpret non-verbal cues such as the tone of their teammates' voices and the body language and expressions on their faces to determine how others in the team were feeling.

Reinforcing this observation, teams that showcased high levels of social sensitivity did very well on an experiment known as *Reading the mind in the Eyes*.

The experiment involves showing someone photos of people's eyes and asking the participant to try to describe what the person in the photo might be thinking or feeling.

Members of high-performing teams were able to detect when their teammates were feeling upset or left out, whilst those from the lower-performing teams seemed to have less empathy and sensitivity towards their colleagues. They showed sensitivity to each other's moods and were comfortable sharing personal stories and speaking openly about their feelings and emotions.

In other words, they were able to build a more personal connection with each other, build stronger levels of empathy and lift the performance of the overall team.

Advice. Take a walk in your teammates' shoes

Quoting directly from the classic book *To Kill a Mockingbird*, "You never really get to know a person until you walk around in their shoes."

Work shadowing and temporary job swaps are a great way of understanding the day-to-day experiences and even challenges of others in your team. The empathy built from such exercises can go a long way to strengthening relationships and more collaborative problem solving.

Advice. *This is me* team exercise

Building greater self-awareness is an important steppingstone towards creating a team culture of empathy.

For both you as a leader and others in the team—understanding your strengths and limitations, your personality styles, how you show up, what motivates you or turns you off; these are key to gaining a more informed perspective on how you can bring value to the team.

Taking the second step to reveal and have an open team discussion on what you each discovered about yourselves from the self-awareness exercise opens up the possibilities of identifying opportunities on how you can support, complement and strengthen how you operate as a team.

A simple but effective exercise to make a start with building greater self-awareness as a team is for each person to write down and subsequently discuss the answer to the following questions:

1. I'm great at...
2. I need to get better at...
3. You can get the best out of me by...
4. You will see the worst of me if...

There are also good online resources such as Myers Briggs personality tests and HBDI exercises that incorporate psychology and behavioural science to get more in-depth personality and behavioural insights to have a richer understanding of you as an individual.

CHAPTER 2.
TRUST AND BE
TRUSTWORTHY

"You can't make your own brain release oxytocin, you can just give that gift to somebody else."

Paul J. Zak

Trust is ranked so highly when it comes to employee engagement in the workplace that it makes up two-thirds of the criteria used by The Great Place to Work Institute and Fortune who produce the 100 Best Companies to Work For. Their own research has shown that "trust between managers and employees is the primary defining characteristic of the very best workplaces."

Professor Paul J Zak, an American neuro-economist and a leading expert on Trust and the application of neuroscience to build high-performing organisations, was able to successfully derive a mathematical relationship between trust and performance. However, he wanted to go deeper and answer the fundamental question of *Why do two people trust each other in the first place*?

His journey to discovering this question is detailed in his 2017 HBR article "The Neuroscience of Trust."

As he illustrates in the article, it was in one of his earlier research experiments that he noticed that rodents released a brain chemical called oxytocin to signal that another animal is safe to approach. This was the lightbulb moment when Professor Zak began to ponder that surely this must be the case for humans too, and there must be an equivalent neurological signal that indicates that we should trust someone. Hence he began his pursuit to prove or disprove his hypothesis.

In order to measure trust and trustworthiness objectively, his team used a strategic decision task developed by researchers from the lab of Vernon Smith, a Nobel laureate in economics whereby a participant (A) chooses an amount of money to send to a stranger (B) via computer[1]. This was in the knowledge that the amount of money sent would triple in value by the time participant B received it. As an example, £3 sent by participant A would triple in value and participant B would receive £9.

The other important piece of information is that participant A was well aware that participant B may choose to share whatever they deemed reasonable and send it back to participant A. Alternatively participant B could also decide not to share any of the spoils at all! Neither participant was told anything about what the study was about so as to ensure there was no influence over their decisions.

After a number of experiments conducted by Professor Zak and his team, the results showed that the more money participant B received from participant A (the sender) the higher the levels of oxytocin produced by participant B. Put another way, the more money received by participant B the higher the perceived trust or trustworthiness in participant A.

Taking this research beyond the lab and into the workplace, Professor Zak found that a culture of trust was a critical feature of high-performing teams and organisations. The studies showed that employees in high-trust organisations were more productive, had higher levels of energy, collaborated better with their colleagues, and stayed with their employers longer than people working at low-trust companies.

Compared with people at low-trust companies, his

research showed that people at high-trust companies reported: 74% less stress, 106% more energy at work, 50% higher productivity, 13% fewer sick days, 76% more engagement, 29% more satisfaction with their lives, 40% less burnout. (2)

Advice. Be intentional about building relationships

Keith Ferrazzi, author of the New York bestselling book *Never Eat Alone* describes relationship building through the lens of what he calls the *Intimacy Pyramid*. If you imagine a pyramid—the higher you are on the pyramid the greater the levels of trust and strength of your relationship with others.

Viewing relationship building through the lens of "what I can get from this exchange" results in a more transactional and lower-trust relationship dynamic, as represented at the bottom of the intimacy pyramid.

Ferrazzi explains that in order to move up the pyramid and build meaningful relationships, it requires a shift in mindset from "What can I get?" to "What can I do for others?" This means being of service to your team more times than they are to you. In other words, supporting them through their most challenging projects and day-to-day issues as well as being the first to celebrate their successes.

It also means showing a genuine interest in finding out more about your colleagues—their passions, interests, likes and dislikes, however recognising that trust works both ways and therefore requires self-disclosure and vulnerability from you first. The more you are willing to reveal pieces of your life outside of work, the more willing your team will be to do so as well.

Ultimately, the higher you are able to get towards the tip of the intimacy pyramid with your team the stronger the relationship you will have with your team and the higher the level of trust you will share with each other.

Advice. It's always the right time to ask for help

In Amy Edmondson's TED talk, *How to turn a group of strangers into a team*, she shares the remarkable story of how on August 5th, 2010 a massive collapse at the San Jose copper mine in Northern Chile left 33 men trapped half a mile below some of the hardest rock in the world. Yet, within 70 days all 33 men were rescued and brought to the surface alive.

This was a significant undertaking requiring hundreds of leaders and their teams across different professions, companies, sectors and nations to come together to solve an incredibly complex issue that had lives at stake.

Despite all the odds being stacked against the mission, on the 17th day they finally managed to break through to the refuge and create a small incision through the rock that enabled the rescuers to create a path wide enough to pass through food and medicine.

Finally, after 53 days of tireless effort, the teams managed to create an even larger hole and design a capsule to rescue the miners one by one.

In Professor Edmondson's popular TED talk, which has been viewed over 2.1 million times, she offers the following explanation of what made the difference in what seemed like mission impossible.

TED talk "How to turn a group of strangers into a team"

"I would say, in a word, it's leadership, but let me be more specific. When teaming works, you can be sure that some leaders, leaders at all levels, have been crystal clear that they don't have the answers.

"Let's call this 'situational humility.' It's appropriate humility. Situational humility combined with curiosity creates a sense of psychological safety that allows you to take risks. They overcame what I like to call the basic human challenge: it's hard to learn if you already know. And, unfortunately, we're hardwired to think we know."

Advice. Be vulnerable first and often. You're not expected to have all the answers

As a new leader, many struggle with the pressure often put on themselves that they should have all the answers; that a strong leader is always in control and unflappable, whatever the situation or circumstance.

By viewing their role through this lens, some leaders will fall into the trap of taking all the burden onto their own shoulders.

This behaviour can also come from a place of good intentions, a desire to protect the team, and not wanting to put pressure on an already stressed and stretched team. However, whilst the underlying motives may be sincere, it can actually have the adverse effect of creating a communication vacuum where their team does not feel engaged or included.

Over time, the disengagement leads to feelings of a lack of trust and disempowerment. The reality, however, is that more often than not the team wants to be engaged, to provide support and may actually have ideas that could really help and add value.

During times of uncertainty or crisis, these feelings of a lack of trust and disengagement can get compounded as team members inevitably experience heightened levels of anxiety and insecurity.

At the turn of the new decade in 2020, no one would have ever predicted the global pandemic that would emerge from COVID-19. At the time of publication of this book approximately three million cases of COVID-19 had been reported in 210 countries and territories, resulting in approximately 200,000 deaths and rising. The COVID-19 pandemic delivered a powerful shock to the global economy amidst deep uncertainty of the full extent of the impact.

It's exactly during times of uncertainty and crisis that a leader's ability to lead with vulnerability is a show of strength. In fact, it's admitting to your teams that you don't have all the answers, and harnessing the power of the team through asking for help and support, that sends strong signals of trust, belonging and safety to your colleagues.

Advice. Listen to your team and be present

"We have two ears and one mouth so that we can listen twice as much as we speak."

Epictetus

In today's busy world of managing multiple priorities and persistent distractions, taking the time to listen to others can often become a de-prioritised communication skill, in favour of moving on to the next important thing. Yet, all the research and evidence show that listening is a critical ingredient of effective communication and building trust.

We may hear what someone is saying, but hearing is a physical ability; listening, on the other hand, is a skill. Trusted leaders are present and in the moment. During the period of time that you have committed to members of your team, make sure that they feel like they are your priority and they have your full attention.

Ensure the interaction between you and your team is a two-way discussion and that you are considered and thoughtful in your responses. This way others will feel they are being listened to and, in turn, inspire trust.

Advice. Ask for feedback

Leaders in high-trust workplaces are willing to admit mistakes when they are wrong and have the humility to ask for help from colleagues. One way of signaling trust to your teams is by asking them for candid and heartfelt feedback.

In Daniel Coyle's book, *The Culture Code*, he suggests that leaders should regularly ask their teams the following three questions:

1. What is the one thing I currently do that you would like me to continue to do?
2. What is the one thing I don't do frequently enough that you would like me to do more often?
3. What can I do to make you more effective?

CHAPTER 3. ENSURE EVERYONE ON THE TEAM HAS A VOICE AT THE TABLE

Project Aristotle, Google's largest study into the secret to building the perfect team, was led by Abeer Dubey (a director within Google's People Analytics division). Dubey brought together some of the company's best organisational psychologists, statisticians, sociologists and engineers, and together they began reviewing half a century of academic studies looking at how teams worked.

As illustrated in the *New York Times Magazine* article *What Google Learned from Its Quest to Build the Perfect Team* it was from this initial research that they developed a set of assessment criteria with which to evaluate the composition of teams within Google. Some of the criteria included levels of social interaction outside the office, interests and hobbies within teams, similarity of educational background, personality types, and the impact of gender diversity in the teams.

Whilst the extensive assessment created an incredible amount of data, the project team struggled to find patterns or evidence that a team's composition made any difference to performance.

It wasn't until the team came across a piece of research based on group norms that things started to make sense and how it was, in fact, the interactions and behaviours within the higher-performing teams that were distinctly different to the lower-performing teams.

Norms are the traditions, behavioural standards and unwritten rules that govern how teams function. As the project Aristotle researchers started to look at the data through this new lens, they noticed specific behaviours that all high-performing teams shared.

One of the first key behavioural observations was

that team members spoke in roughly the same proportion, a phenomenon the research team referred to as equality in distribution of conversational turn asking. Irrespective of the problems that they were trying to solve, everyone in the high-performing teams had spoken roughly the same amount. (3)

Advice. Ensure all ideas are heard and evaluated equally

"There is no correlation between being the best talker and the best ideas."

Susan Cain

The very best ideas and solutions often come from harnessing perspectives from individuals with different experiences and backgrounds.

Often, you'll find when trying to solve problems or coming up with creative solutions teams default to brainstorming. Brainstorming definitely has an important role to play in the workplace; however, what you often find is that 80% of ideas generated come from 20% of the people in the meeting. This can often be compounded where ideas are being discussed remotely or by virtual teams.

An alternative way of encouraging all ideas and perspectives from all team members to be heard, and ultimately get to the best ideas, is to ask team members to write down their ideas on cards, which are then posted on a wall for the rest of the group to discuss and vote on. For teams working remotely, there are some great collaboration tools such as IdeaBoardz that can be used to facilitate this exercise.

Advice: Speak last in meetings

As the most senior person, you may feel compelled to either do the majority of the talking during team meetings or offer your ideas first to get the conversation going. However, consistently being the dominant voice in the room can have the following unintentional effects.

1. You create what is known as the *mirroring effect*, where team members consciously or subconsciously gravitate to the person of authority in the room. Team members either default to either agreeing with everything you say or do not feel safe to challenge and offer a different perspective. Over time, this approach creates disengagement and stifles the richness of the discussion and idea generation process you get from having diverse thinking and perspectives.
2. You impact the confidence and development of the more junior members in your team as they get less opportunities to practice the art of meeting management.

Advice: Set the stage for all the personality types in your team

Within your team you are likely to have a diverse

set of personality types; these may include dominant, expressive, analytical and amiable personalities. If you have members within the team that have dominant or expressive traits, it is important that you ensure you are facilitating the discussion in a way that ensures that all the personality types in the team are heard.

One way is to draw out views and perspectives from the quieter or more reserved team members early on in the meeting. Once they've had a chance to speak up, invite others in the team to contribute.

However, your role in the meeting doesn't stop there; you need to ensure that the equal balance of voices in the room remains consistent throughout. Asking individuals whether they agree with another team member's perspective is a good way of inviting others back into the conversation.

Advice: Encourage dissenting perspectives

In Patrick Lencioni's bestselling leadership book, *The Five Dysfunctions of a Team*, one of the main reasons that teams often don't commit to decisions that are made in the room is due to a lack of constructive conflict and debate leading up to that decision.

Not fully committing to the decision results in individuals lacking a sense of accountability for delivering on what was agreed, and ultimately this has a negative impact on the quality of the results.

Surrounding yourself with people who are willing to disagree with you, and challenge your perspectives and each other, not only allows you to make better and informed decisions but builds a culture of safety and trust where diverse perspectives are encouraged.

CHAPTER 4.
LEAVE TITLES
AND EGOS AT
THE DOOR

P eter Skillman, a veteran of creative product design and engineering, delivered a 2006 TED talk where he introduced a design challenge called the marshmallow challenge.

TED Talk - Peter Skillman - Marshmallow Design Challenge

In his TED talk he describes how over several months, he challenged students across different age groups across the world to build the tallest possible standing out of

    1. twenty pieces of uncooked spaghetti

   2. one yard of transparent tape
   3. one yard of string
   4. one standard-size marshmallow

The only rule was that the marshmallow had to be at the top of the standing structure.

Interestingly, amongst the worst structures built were those constructed by business school students, who on average built not only the shortest structures but the least visually appealing and least stable structures. Surprisingly, the group that produced the highest-standing structures with the more robust and visually diverse and creative designs were, in fact, kindergarten students.

On average, the kindergarteners built structures that averaged 26 inches tall, whilst the business school students built structures that averaged 10 inches or less. (4)

Intrigued to understand this unexpected phenomenon, Skillman observed and analysed the behaviours and social interactions amongst the groups. What he found was that the business school students did a lot more planning and strategising, jockeying for power to understand who was in charge, and trying to figure out if it was okay to challenge ideas.

The kindergarteners, on the other hand, did not know or care who was in charge; happy to take risks, they quickly spotted when something wasn't working, made adjustments whenever necessary and offered each other help.

In Daniel Coyle's book, *The Culture Code*, he provides a fascinating illustration of the behavioural differences between the two groups as follows:

Business School Students.

"The business school students appear to be collaborating, but in fact they are engaged in a process psychologists call status management. They are figuring out where they fit into the larger picture: Who is in charge? Is it okay to criticize someone's idea? What are the rules here? Their interactions appear smooth, but their underlying behaviour is riddled with inefficiency, hesitation, and subtle competition. Instead of focusing on the task, they are navigating their uncertainty about one another. They spend so much time managing status that they fail to grasp the essence of the problem (the marshmallow is relatively heavy, and the spaghetti is hard to secure). As a result, their first efforts often collapse, and they run out of time."

Kindergarten Students.

"The actions of the kindergartners appear disorganised on the surface. But when you view them as a single entity, their behaviour is efficient and effective. They are not competing for status. They stand shoulder to shoulder and work energetically together. They move quickly, spotting problems and offering help. They experiment, take risks, and notice outcomes, which guides them toward effective solutions."

The behaviours exhibited by the kindergarteners have a strong resemblance to the interactions and dynamics from the high-performing Google teams discovered in Project Aristotle. Both sets of groups were working in team environments where there were high levels of psychological safety.

Amy Edmondson, who is the Novartis professor of Leadership at Harvard Business School, explains psychological safety as, "a belief that one will not be punished or humiliated for speaking up with ideas, questions, concerns or mistakes."

A more in-depth insight into psychological safety can be found on her TED talk, Building a psychologically safe workplace and her book The Fearless Organisazation: Creating Psychological Safety in the Workplace for Learning, Innovation and Growth

TED Talk, Building a psychologically safe workplace

These social interactions were also highly reminiscent of the behaviours Professor Alex Pentland from MIT covered in his book *Social Physics,* where he shares his in-depth research of communities and organisations in his search for the most successful and innovative teams.

1. Everyone in group talks in equal measures - keeping engages short
2. High levels of eye contact - energetic exchanges
3. Members communicate directly with one another - not just with the team leader
4. Side or back channel conversations happen within the team
5. Members periodically break - think, explore and bring information back within the team to share with others

Advice. Ask your team how psychologically safe they feel in the team

How do leaders go about understanding how psychologically safe their team members feel? Ask them!
Periodically check in on your team to find out how safe they feel and what could enhance their feeling of safety.

Amy Edmonson developed a simple yet effective questionnaire that leaders can use with their teams on psychological safety and other team dynamics.

1. When someone makes a mistake on this team, it is often held against him or her
2. In this team, it is easy to discuss difficult issues and problems
3. In this team, people are sometimes rejected

for being different
4. It is completely safe to take a risk on this team
5. It is difficult to ask other members of this team for help
6. Members of this team value and respect each other's contributions

Advice. Replace blame with curiosity

During high-pressure situations, where there can be tendencies for tensions to be high and fuses short, this can lead to finger pointing and blame both from the team leader and between teams. Over time, it has the effect of eroding trust and effective collaboration.

Dr John Gottman's extensive research on resolving conflict highlights that blame and criticism inevitably and reliably escalate conflict, leading to defensiveness and eventually to disengagement. In a team that lacks psychological safety, these negative behaviours are even more prevalent.

So it's important that leaders adopt a curious and learning mindset and approach, recognising that in most situations they won't have all the facts. They need to be thoughtful of how they approach conflict and role-model the right behaviours to diffuse and enable teams to move forward. For if you believe that you already know what the other person is thinking then you are not ready to have a conversation.

The alternative to blame is curiosity, and one way to achieve this is by being deliberate about the language that is used during these situations. Specifically, language that signals curiosity, as opposed to emphasising blame. Some examples of the type of language that can be used during these times of pressure include:

"Tell me more."

"How can I help and support you?"

"I imagine that there are multiple factors at play. Why don't we work through these together?"

"What would be a good result here? How could we get there together?"

CHAPTER 5.
LEVEL THE
PLAYING FIELD

"We might all be playing the same game, but a bumpy pitch is not the same as a smooth one."

Joanna Abeyie, MBE

Like many others in the world, throughout my school life and career in the corporate world, I've been one of the few if not only person of colour in the room. For a long time, I had become a master of blending in and was highly alert to and conscious of how I was or might be perceived. In fact, my accent became less and less Kenyan; I became more polished and my interests expanded into areas that I wasn't actually that interested in.

Early in my career, I remember that I would turn up early to meetings and try to seat myself as far away from the middle of the conversation as possible, so that I could blend in and appear less threatening. I simply wasn't showing up as my full and best self; instead, it was a guarded version of me.

A few weeks later, I walked into one of our regular meetings and one of the senior executives – a tall, larger-than-life and gregarious black Caribbean man – hollered at me, "Nelson, I've saved you a spot next to me."

Every meeting following, he would save that spot next to him, and over time my confidence developed, and it showed in my contributions to the meetings. I felt included and that my voice and perspectives mattered. He was the first successful man of colour I'd met who quite literally was bringing his authentic self to work and was an example of how being himself wasn't holding him back.

More importantly, he created and fostered an environment where everyone under his care felt safe and empowered to be themselves and bring divergent perspectives and ideas. Under his leadership, his teams and organisations were consistently among the highest performing and he went on to become one of the first black partners from the division— not to mention, at one of the most prestigious investment banks in the world at the time.

Advice. Be an inclusive leader

He exemplified what it meant to be an inclusive leader, recognising that people are complex and have multiple dimensions to them, including their backgrounds, experiences and personalities; also that barriers and glass ceilings show up differently, and as a leader it is their role to create a level playing field where individuals are able to show up and compete with their peers on a level playing field.

As a leader you can start by asking your team:

- What challenges they might be experiencing
- How they may be being excluded
- Whether team dynamics are holding them back or if it's the wider culture of the organisation
- What barriers they may keep bumping into as a result of their backgrounds

This can be achieved through surveys and focus group sessions in a psychologically safe setting to get the depth and richness of the experiences.

Other areas for leaders to lead more inclusively include:

Encourage and include topics on diversity and inclusion as a regular standing agenda item within team meetings.

Create a more inclusive and flexible career path so as to enable career success for all talent such as working parents and individuals with disabilities.

Explore opportunities to make team-building and social events more inclusive. More consideration to be made around activities, venues and timings to ensure no one in the team feels excluded or uncomfortable.

CHAPTER 6. UNDERSTAND WHAT MOTIVATES YOUR TEAM

You need not see what someone is doing to know if it is their vocation; you have only to watch their eyes:

A cook mixing a sauce.
A surgeon making a primary incision.
A clerk completing a bill of lading.

They all wear the same rapt expression, forgetting themselves in a function.

How beautiful it is, that eye-on-the-object look.

W.H. Auden

I t was summer term at junior school in Nairobi when I was first introduced to the game of cricket. I was around 10 years old. Living in let's say the more modest part of town cricket wasn't exactly a game that my neighbourhood friends ever heard of, let alone played. Football was what got our competitive juices going and Maradona and Pele were our heroes!

So as a 10-year-old football enthusiast, the game of cricket seemed somewhat awkward, slow and way too *posh* for someone like me. However, the more I played cricket the more I realised I had a knack for the game, and I grew to appreciate the skill level, both physically and mentally, that was required.

I'd spend countless hours with my teammates practicing and honing our skills and experience. In those moments, it was as if time stood still—I was so absorbed in what we were doing that nothing else in the world mattered.

Mihaly Csikszentmihaly, the Hungarian-American psychologist noted for his research into happiness, describes this experience as *Flow*. In an interview with *Wired Magazine*, Csikszentmihaly described flow as "being completely involved in an activity for its own sake. The ego falls away. Time flies.

Every action, movement, and thought follows inevitably from the previous one, like playing jazz. Your whole being is involved, and you're using your skills to the utmost."

Whenever my teammates and I stepped onto the field, the overwhelming drivers that motivated us to bring out the best in us were that we were playing for each other and representing our school and all the pupils and teachers that supported us. We all felt like we were playing for something greater than ourselves.

The Japanese have this word, *Ikigai*', which translates as having a *direction or purpose in life* or a *reason for being*—the French equivalent is *raison d'être*. It has also been described as *entailing actions of devoting oneself to pursuits that one enjoys and is associated with feelings of accomplishment and fulfillment* within the eudaimonic well-being circles.

In Dan Buettner's 2009 TED talk, *How to live to be 100+*, the *National Geographic* reporter studied the ikigai philosophy of the inhabitants of the Okinawa. Okinawa, located south of mainland Japan, is a group of islands known as the *land of the immortals*. Okinawans are known to not only have the longest lifespans in the world but the highest number of centurions in the world.

In his research, Buettner concluded that ikigai was one of the reasons for Okinawan's longevity. In the bestselling book, *Ikigai: The Japanese secret to a long and happy life*, authors Hector Garcia and Francesco Miralles explain that activities that allow one to feel ikigai are never forced on an individual; they are spontaneous and always undertaken willingly, giving the individual satisfaction and a sense of meaning of life.

Advice. Align career goals to what drives your team members

According to Gallup's meta-analysis of decades of data, it shows that high levels of engagement are defined largely as having a strong connection with one's work and colleagues, feeling like a real contributor, and enjoying ample chances to learn—consistently leading to positive outcomes for both individuals and organisations. The rewards include higher productivity, better-quality products, and increased profitability.

The link between positive career experiences and business performance is also supported by over a decade of research. For example, one study published in an issue of *Personnel Review* found a clear tie between more positive employee ratings and several organisational performance measures, including operating margin, revenue per employee, and return on company assets.

In Daniel Pink's book, *Drive - The Surprising Truth of What Motivates Us*, he draws upon 50 years of study into behavioural science to deduce that human beings have three psychological needs—Autonomy, Competence, and Relatedness. When these needs are satisfied, we are motivated, productive, and happy.

As individuals, we have a unique set of strengths, personality traits, career ambitions, and goals that drive and motivate us. The more we can do work that we feel we are good at, that compliments the way we like to solve problems and moves us closer to our future career goals, the more motivated we will be to deliver our best work.

Career frameworks often prescribe generic and static corporate expectations of a role within the organisation (e.g. role responsibilities, targets, competency expectations) with very little consideration (if any) of the individual's own personal goals and motivations.

Career frameworks should serve as guidelines to the expected outcomes linked to "good" performance in a role. However, how these outcomes are achieved should be a collaborative and personalised discussion between the career manager and individual.

Leaders play a critical role as influencers on the careers of those under their care, which means they have a responsibility to ensure that they are taking the time to understand each individual on their teams—and subsequently to identify the work and opportunities that play to their natural strengths and will contribute to their future career goals.

Advice. Recognise and reward your team in the right way

As a cricket team we achieved a fair amount of success, winning several championships. However, when I look back at the memories that stood out, it wasn't the awards and accolades that we achieved that I recall. In fact, it was the hours and hours spent practising at the nets, the moments when I needed to hold my nerve and bowl that maiden over, bouncing back from losses, the bonds and friendships I made with my teammates and coach. The real reward came from the satisfaction of playing cricket. The accolades were just a bonus.

That was what inspired and motivated us. As Simon Sinek describes it, that was our WHY.

Financial rewards and accolades are what Daniel Pink describes in his book *Drive* as "Extrinsic Motivators". The achievement of accolades and financial success certainly brings enjoyment, but that feeling of elation is usually short-lived and the reality of one's' day-to-day kicks back in.

As we enter the era of a multi-generational workforce, employees have a different take and outlook on what drives and inspires them than what was commonly accepted as motivating in the past.

Behavioural science tells us that we change our behaviour when given gifts that reinforce actions and goals, but research also shows that financial reward is not the straightforward motivator that companies often assume it is. In fact, too much extrinsic reward can *lessen* internal motivation if perceived as controlling.

There is a transition away from extrinsic motivators (such as money, titles, corporate logos, the allure of an attractive final salary and pension scheme) towards career experiences and opportunities that enable employees to pursue their intrinsic motivators.

Here are a few of the intrinsic motivators that keep employees engaged that as a leader you should pursue when looking to motivate your team:

- Solving problems that your team find enjoyable and care about
- Doing work that they are good at and where they can grow and develop both professionally and personally
- Doing mission and purpose-driven work that is making a difference and impact
- Being able to be authentic and bring their full and best self to work
- Having a sense of belonging and feeling part of something bigger than themselves
- Being able to have a successful and fulfilling career and a successful and fulfilling personal life

Advice. Give your team autonomy

"Don't tell people how to do things, tell them what to do and let them surprise you with their results."

George S. Patton

In behavioural science, the *autonomy bias* tells us that we have an innate need to be agents of our own lives. In the context of work, *autonomy* is the ability to direct your approach to work and your career path.

According to Pink, "By rethinking traditional ideas of control – regular office hours, dress codes, numerical targets, and so on – organizations can increase staff autonomy, build trust, and improve innovation and creativity." In other words, if you focus on creating the conditions and environments for your teams to do their best work, this will create a happier, productive, and empowered team.

Advice. Align career goals to the purpose of the organisation

The Hungarian-American psychologist Mihaly Csikszentmihalyi famously said, "One cannot lead a life that is truly excellent without feeling that one belongs to something greater and more permanent than oneself."

Our beliefs (ideas that you hold to be true) and values (what is important to you) are core to decision-making. This facet of human nature dictates that people are more motivated to try to excel in a company that they believe in and that shares their beliefs and values. Organisations with a clearly defined mission behind WHY they do what they do, supported by a strong set of company values, can help to cultivate a sense of belonging for employees.

In behavioural science, there is a cognitive bias called the *Ikea Effect*, which highlights that it is in our human nature to believe something is of greater value to us if we have contributed in making or creating it. The name derives from the name of the Swedish manufacturer and furniture retailer IKEA, which sells many furniture products that require customers to assemble the parts.

One way that as a leader you can engage and align your team to the purpose of the organisation as a whole is to challenge your team to think about suggestions for how they as individuals and as a collective team can show up to support the purpose. That can be in the priorities of the team or even an adjustment in values and behaviours. By engaging your team in this way, co-creating changes in the ways of working, you will motivate your team to be aligned to the organisation's purpose.

Leaders need to communicate how the work that their teams are doing is moving the organisation towards its overall mission. It requires a deliberate focus on ensuring career frameworks are designed to support their teams in defining career goals that directly and clearly contribute to the overall mission of the organisation. Doing so injects a sense of purpose into their team's work, making them significantly more likely to evoke greater enthusiasm.

CHAPTER 7.
HOW YOU COMMUNICATE MATTERS MORE THAN EVER

As a new leader, your ability to influence others towards a team vision, or convince them to buy into a new way of thinking, requires a compelling communication style. Subconsciously, however, there are several factors that influence whether or not others decide to embrace your message, be indifferent to it, or even reject it.

Do they believe you care about what you're saying?

Do they trust what you are saying? Do they trust

you?

Are they interested in what you have to say?

Do they understand and follow what you are saying?

Advice. Speak with authenticity

One of the traits that differentiate between the truly great communicators of past and present is the authenticity that they bring to their message. They become their message and it's this realness and integrity that makes us want to believe and buy into what they are saying. It's this genuine authenticity that sets them apart from their peers.

They speak with passion, conviction and enthusiasm and their audience gets a brief window into their soul and authentic self. Their voice then serves as the vehicle to translate this authenticity to their audience.

Advice. Be a storyteller

"It's not what you say, it's how you make them feel."

Frank Luntz

Whether it's a good story (e.g. brief history lesson of the topic at hand), interesting fact (e.g. a less-known statistic), or even a well-thought-out analogy (a relevant personal experience), when carefully weaved into the message these are what bring ideas to life, that make what we say memorable and believable.

Advice. Keep your message simple

Make brevity your best friend. Forget about verbose and illustrative language and phrases that more often than not confuse your audiences—use short sentences or, even better, use a picture, which can often be worth a thousand words.

Advice. Communicate frequently and widely

According to Professor Zak (author of the HBR article *The Neuroscience of Trust*), only 40% of employees report that they are well informed about their company's goals, strategies, and tactics. This uncertainty about the company's direction leads to chronic stress, which inhibits the release of oxytocin and undermines teamwork. Openness is the antidote.

CHAPTER 8. GO THE EXTRA MILE TO HIRE THE BEST TALENT

On paper, he was destined to be one of the greats. Attending high school in San Diego, he excelled at numerous sports, in particular baseball, football and basketball. From an early age, scouts were in awe of his talent with interest from many prestigious universities, including Stanford University who tried to recruit him on a joint baseball-football scholarship.

Yet, in spite of all the hype, his playing career failed to meet the glittering expectations of those scouts, many of which projected that he was to be one of the stars of baseball.

This is the story of Billy Beane, whose life and career was documented in Michael Lewis' 2003 book, *Moneyball: The Art of Winning an Unfair Game.*

Now, whilst Billy Beane never made it as a star player, he did achieve incredible success, notably as the general manager of Oakland Athletics (the Major League Baseball team).

Arguably, his greatest achievement and contribution to the sport was transforming the value placed on talent and the formula used to build successful and high-performing teams. Many of Billy Beane's talent philosophies transcend industries and are relevant outside of the baseball stadium.

His legacy-defining decision was to turn to Sabermetrics – an analytical, evidence-based performance capability – to make more informed decisions around the value and potential placed on player talent.

This unorthodox approach (as thought of at the time) flew in the face of decades of collective 'wisdom' of the baseball establishment and insiders (including players, managers, scouts and coaches) that favoured subjective evaluation of potential rather than objective competency-based evaluations.

However, with a fraction of the budget of his rivals, in the 2002/2003 season he built a team that secured a record 20-game winning streak and took them to the playoffs. The team's 2002 campaign ranks among the most famous in franchise history.

Advice. Reassess how you select talent for your team

On paper, the new look team that Billy picked was underwhelming—at least to many of the seasoned 'experts' that is. To them it lacked the player CV and brand power that one would associate with a team in the major leagues.

However, Billy had been deliberate and forensic in identifying the specific capabilities and attributes he needed to build a winning team and to pick the best available players that possessed those competencies, placing far less emphasis on the brand or prestige of the teams they had played for before.

Innovative solutions are coming out of organisations such as HackerRank, Knack, Nottx, and Headlight Labs, which place greater emphasis on assessing a candidate's competencies, skills, critical thinking, values and personal qualities.

This is in contrast to some of the more established and traditional capabilities (such as the traditional CV), which (particularly when used in isolation) arguably place more emphasis on education attainment, qualifications, occupational accomplishments and institutional pedigree, giving way to potential unconscious bias and the increased risk of missing out on high-potential talent.

Advice. Challenge your biases

Raised by a single mum, both her dad and elder sister had died by the time she was three years old. Growing up in the Ugandan slums of Katwe, she was surrounded by poverty and had no choice but to drop out of school because her family could no longer afford to send her. It was a choice between education and going hungry. Literally living day to day, she sold maize in the Katwe street market. One day, she followed her brother to an after-school outreach program run by a gentleman by the name of Robert Katende. It was there that she discovered the game of chess.

Mr. Katende, who had also grown up in the slums as a boy, looked beyond the outward appearance of the young lady in front of him and could see her incredible potential. Introducing her to the game of chess and investing in her potential literally changed the course of her life. The investment paid off and she became the first female player in Ugandan chess history to win an Olympiad title. She was eventually able to return to school to continue her education and attend university in the US.

Those of you who have read the book or watched the film *Queen of Katwe*, you will recognise this inspiring person as Phiona Mutesi.

British chess journalist John Saunders made the following observation about Phiona's chess game, which brings to light the significant influence that one's social environment can play in the lottery of life.

"...placed in the context of her environmental and educational deprivation, her achievement reaching such a level has been awe-inspiring."

Making hiring decisions, identifying the individual in your team to lead that high-profile project, and promotions may be some or all of your responsibilities as a new leader. Making the right choice also requires you to challenge your potential biases. Everyone holds unconscious beliefs about various social and identity groups, which stem from a natural tendency to organise social worlds by categorising.

Challenging one's own bias as a leader means rethinking one's perspective of what talent looks and sounds like and getting more expansive and innovative on who gets the opportunity to join and progress in your teams.

CHAPTER 9. FINAL ADVICE. LOOK AFTER PEOPLE ON THE WAY UP

My brother and I were raised by a single mum in Nairobi, Kenya. We had little in the way of material things, particularly in the early part of our childhood. We all lodged in a single room in a modest apartment in the humble part of Nairobi. However, what my brother and I lacked in material things was outweighed by life lessons and love from our mother.

My mum had an unwavering vision for her kids that the right education was going to be the key to unlocking a better future for my brother and me. She made the difficult decision to use the little money that she'd saved up to put me through the first year of private primary school, not knowing where the money would come from for the following year's school fees. Friends and family were very critical of her choice, as this was seen as reckless and inconsiderate.

I remember like it was yesterday, my mum sitting me down before my first day of school to prepare and explain to me that I'd be going to a school where I would be different. The other kids would be driven in expensive cars to school (whilst I would be walking the 45 minute journey to school). Their uniforms would be new and they'd have the latest and trendy sports kit (mine would be mostly second hand). They would have big houses and travel abroad during the holiday break.

As she came to the end of her talk, she said one thing that has always stuck with me - "but make sure you keep your head up high because you know what, it's your difference that is and will always be your greatest strength".

Things got tough for a little while, but she never questioned or regretted her choice. In the end, it ended up being a wise investment decision as the school offered me a significant bursary that relieved a lot of the financial pressure on the family.

In school, sports and music were my passion and consumed all my free time and thoughts. We could never afford to have piano lessons or pay the fees to join a sports club, but there was a sports teacher (who was also the school deputy head) who invested a lot of his personal time to ensure I could pursue my passions.

He would open the music room an hour before school officially started where I taught myself to play the piano. He would keep the sports facilities open for an hour after school and would often join me in a game of cricket, football or rugby. After a school event such as a sports match, he would make an unscheduled detour to drop me off at home (so I didn't have to walk home in the evening). He was my first true mentor, coach and sponsor.

At the age of 13 I was in the final year of primary school and we again had the dilemma of how we were going to afford to pay for my secondary school. One summer's afternoon, we were playing against a rival school at cricket. Little did I know that it was a day that was going to change the course of my life forever.

After the game, a parent from the rival school that we played against walked over to me to congratulate us on the win. I didn't think any more of it, but the next morning my sports teacher called me into the staffroom to say that the parent I'd met the previous day was in fact one of the wealthiest businessmen in Kenya.

They'd been talking about me after the game, and

the businessman was offering to sponsor me to go over to the UK to study for my secondary school. It still seems surreal when I think about it. This was a complete stranger with zero ties or relationship to me or my family but his gift changed the course and fortune of my life forever.

Looking back, the investments that these individuals made in me (their counsel, advice, time, belief and kindness) have shaped the person I have become today and informed many of my core values.

As leaders, many of us have been fortunate enough to have mentors, sponsors, friends and colleagues that have played their part in our success. Make sure you send the elevator back down—invest in the future; become the opportunity maker; provide the platform; offer the advice; give up some of your personal time and inspire others.

In 2019, I was speaking with my childhood sponsor and he shared some wise words:

> *"An old adage for you, Nelson, that I live by.*
> *Look after the people on the way up because you*
> *might just meet them on the way down."*

———

REFERENCES

Books

García, H & Miralles, F. (2017). Ikigai: The Japanese secret to a long and happy life. Hutchinson

Lewis, M. (2004) Moneyball: The Art of Winning an Unfair Game. W. W. Norton & Company

Ferrazzi, K. (2014). Never Eat Alone: And Other Secrets to Success, One Relationship at a Time. Penguin

Coyle, D. (2019). The Culture Code: The Secrets of Highly Successful Groups. Random House Business (4) citation references to book

Lencioni, P. (2002) The Five Dysfunctions of a Team: A Leadership Fable. John Wiley & Sons

Schmidt, E., Rosenberg, J., Eagle, A. (2020). Trillion Dollar Coach: The Leadership Handbook of Silicon Valley's Bill Campbell. John Murray

Harper, L. (2010). To Kill A Mockingbird. Arrow

TED Talks

Edmondson, A. (2014) Building a psychologically safe workplace

Buettner, D. (2010) How to live to be 100+

Edmondson, A. (2018). How to turn a group of strangers into a team

Skillman, P (2006). Marshmallow Design Challenge by Peter Skillman

Articles

Duhigg, C. (2016) What Google Learned from Its Quest to Build the Perfect Team. The New York Times Magazine
(3) citation references to article

Zak, P. (2017) The Neuroscience of Trust. Harvard Business Review
(1) (2) citation references to article

ABOUT THE AUTHOR

Nelson Derry

For over 15 years Nelson has been helping leaders unlock the potential of their teams through adopting high performing habits and behaviours, and building cultures of trust, purpose and belonging.

An award-winning executive, he has been recognised by the Financial Times and EMPower as one of the Top 30 Future Leaders in the U.K. for contributions to workplace inclusion and talent management.

Nelson is a thought leader on the topics of high performing teams, organisational culture, leadership and professional development, and regularly contributes content on social media and at industry conferences.

Always open to building new professional relationships, you can reach Nelson on his LinkedIn handle -

www.linkedin.com/in/nelson-derry

Printed in Great Britain
by Amazon

11644537R00041